God's Little Christmas Book

HONOR
B O O K S

Tulsa, Oklahoma

God's Little Christmas Book
ISBN 1-56292-359-5
Copyright 1997 © by Honor Books
P. O. Box 55388
Tulsa, Oklahoma 74155

Introduction

That wonderful night in Bethlehem, God declared His love for mankind when His Sacred Covenant became flesh and blood — Emmanuel!

No wonder angels rejoiced, shepherds bowed in awe, and wise men traveled so far to give gifts! They all recognized the significance of this Holy Birth, which was hidden in Scripture from the beginning of time.

Through beauty and diversity, *God's Little Christmas Book* is designed to create a sense of celebration and praise for God's gracious gift — our Lord and Savior Jesus Christ!

To the Reader

We hope you will enjoy *God's Little Christmas Book* as much as we have enjoyed compiling it. May it enrich your own holiday traditions and leave you with a fresh appreciation for our Lord Jesus Christ.

As you unfold the pages of this book, you will see that the heart of this book is drawn from Scripture, but we have also gathered readings from a broad range of Christmas folklore, legends, and traditions that have been passed down through the ages.

In doing so, it has been our intention to express the depth with which cultures throughout the world have embraced God's greatest gift to mankind.

We hope that *God's Little Christmas Book* will stir the embers of generosity and kindness toward all men the world over all year through.

Table of Contents

Angels & Advent

God sent the angel Gabriel to the Galilean village of Nazareth to a virgin engaged to be married to a man descended from David....the angel assured her, "Mary, you have nothing to fear. God has a surprise for you: You will become pregnant and give birth to a son and call his name Jesus.

He will be great, be called 'Son of the Highest.' The Lord God will give him the throne of his father David;

He will rule Jacob's house forever — no end, ever, to his kingdom."

— Luke 1:26,27,30,31 THE MESSAGE

Angels & Advent

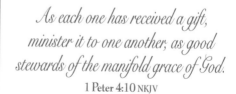

Our first Christmas gift is the Gift of gifts, Jesus Himself, the Son of God. Without Christ there is no Christmas, for a Christmas without Christ is meaningless.

But the tiny Babe in the crib has conquered all hearts. His birthday has become a day of joy for the whole world. It is not difficult to see, therefore, why events which fell on this birthday or happenings related to the sacred festival are of intense interest to every lover of the Christ Child.

As each one has received a gift, minister it to one another, as good stewards of the manifold grace of God.
1 Peter 4:10 NKJV

How can we explain the mysterious fascination that hovers over every Christmas season? Is it not that all men inherently sense that Jesus continues to show the gifts of His grace on all mankind?

The antiphon of the Magnificat for the second vespers of Christmas Day best expresses the joy in our hearts:

"This day Christ is born; this day the Saviour hath appeared; this day the angels sing on earth, the archangels rejoice; this day the just exult, saying: Glory to God in the highest, alleluia."

Holy, holy, holy, Lord God Almighty, Who was and is and is to come!

Revelation 4:8 NKJV

13

Angels & Advent

Good news from heaven the angels bring,

Glad tidings to the earth they sing:

To us this day a

child is given,

To crown us with

the joy of heaven.

—Martin Luther

This Good News was promised long ago by God's prophets in the Old Testament.

Romans 1:2 TLB

The practice of singing Christmas carols appears to be almost as old as the celebration of the day itself. In the first days of the Church, the bishops sang carols on Christmas Day, recalling the songs sung by the angel at the birth of Christ.

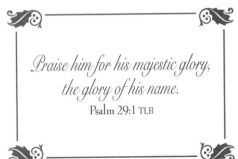

Praise him for his majestic glory, the glory of his name.
Psalm 29:1 TLB

Christmas is a "Mary" Time

Mary was born in the city of Nazareth. Her father, Joachim, hailed from Nazareth in Galilee, while Anna, her mother, came from Bethlehem. They had made a vow that if the Lord blessed them with offspring, they would yield the child to the service of the Lord and thus Mary was brought up in the temple.

Rejoice, highly favored one, the Lord is with you; blessed are you among women!
Luke 1:28 NKJV

God sent the angel Gabriel to announce to Mary her role in the Incarnation of Christ.

Then, having been instructed and assured by the Angel of the Lord, Joseph took Mary as his wife and knew her not until she had brought forth JESUS, her firstborn son.

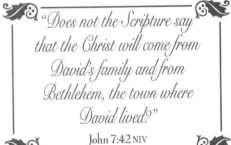

"Does not the Scripture say that the Christ will come from David's family and from Bethlehem, the town where David lived?"

John 7:42 NIV

17

Angels & Advent

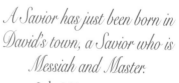

Angels from the realms of glory,

Wing your flight o'er all the earth;

Ye, who sang creation's story,

Now proclaim
Messiah's birth:

Come and worship!

Come and worship!

Worship Christ, the
newborn King!

— James Montgomery

*A Savior has just been born in
David's town, a Savior who is
Messiah and Master.*
Luke 2:11 THE MESSAGE

In Italy, the *Presepio* or *crib* is as characteristic of Christmas as the tree in Germany.

Every home, even the poorest, has a Presepio of some kind, and the churches have very elaborate ones. The people place humble gifts of nuts and apples in the hands of the life-sized figures.

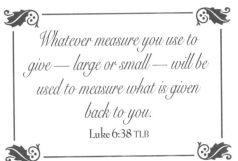

Whatever measure you use to give — large or small — will be used to measure what is given back to you.

Luke 6:38 TLB

Angels & Advent

For centuries the voice of the bell has been heeded with reverence on all occasions and Christmas is no exception. The joyous peals of bells and melodious strains of chimes, welcoming the birth of the Saviour, are happy features of the Christmas festival.

In many places the clang of bells is heard for hours on Christmas Eve and early Christmas morning, carrying aloft the message of the angels: "Glory to God in the highest."

At once the angel was joined by a huge angelic choir singing God's praises:
"Glory to God in the heavenly heights."
Luke 2:13,14 THE MESSAGE

In medieval times, the bells were tolled for one hour before midnight on Christmas Eve.

The purpose of the tolling it was said, was to give the powers of darkness notice of the approaching birth of the Saviour. In England it was called, "Tolling the Devil's Knell" to signify the triumph of Christ's birth.

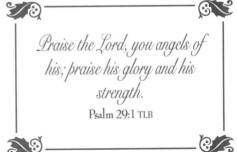

Praise the Lord, you angels of his; praise his glory and his strength.
Psalm 29:1 TLB

21

Angels & Advent

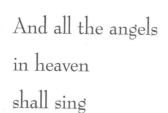

And all the angels in heaven shall sing

On Christmas Day, on Christmas Day,

And all the angels

in heaven

shall sing

On Christmas Day

in the morning.

*Who is able to number his hosts
of angels?*
Job 25:3 TLB

A German legend tells that on Christmas Eve the careful listener can hear the bells of all the churches, chapels, monasteries, and cities destroyed by war chiming in unison.

My sheep hear My voice, and I know them, and they follow Me.
John 10:27 NKJV

23

Angels & Advent

The *four* weeks of Advent preceding Christmas represent the *four* great prophesies concerning the coming of the Saviour in the Old Testament.

The first promise:
In Paradise after the fall of our first parents, Adam and Eve, God promised that the woman's Son would one day crush the head of the serpent.

He is sending us a Mighty Savior from the royal line of his servant David, just as he promised through his holy prophets long ago.
Luke 1:69, 70 TLB

The second promise: God promised the childless Abraham that he would become the father of a new nation and in his seed all the nations of the earth would be blessed.

The third promise: From Abraham's seed, through the family of David, the Saviour of the world would be born.

The fourth promise: Out of David's family, would come the virgin mother of Christ. "A Virgin will bring forth a Son and His name shall be called Emmanuel, God with us."

> *It is the Good News about his Son, Jesus Christ our Lord, who came as a human baby, born into King David's royal family line.*
>
> Romans 1:3 TLB

25

Angels & Advent

J oy to the world, the Lord is come!
Let earth receive her King;
Let ev'ry heart prepare Him room
And heav'n and
   nature sing,
And heav'n and
   nature sing,
And heav'n,
   And heav'n and
   nature sing.
— Isaac Watts

I will praise you with great joy.
Psalm 63:5 TLB

X_{mas}

During the Holiday Season, it has become commonplace to see an "X" replacing "Christ" in the word "Christmas." This is viewed by many as a crass attempt to separate the Savior from the season's festivities.

In fact, X is an abbreviation for Christ. It originated from the Greek letter X (chi) beginning the name of Christ (the Anointed).

Those who love Christ can find cause to rejoice even when urged to have a "Merry Xmas!"

The Spirit of the Lord is upon Me, Because He has anointed Me.
Luke 4:18 NKJV

27

Angels & Advent

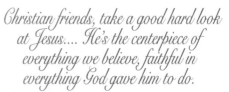

Anticipation, the Joy of Advent: Special family traditions can accentuate each day with Christmas joy.

· **Jesse Tree:** Design 24 symbolic ornaments for Christ's Old Testament spiritual heritage/ancestors. Each December day hang one of the ornaments on the Jesse Tree. On Christmas Day; transfer all 24 ornaments to the Christmas tree, symbolizing fulfillment of the Messianic promise.

Christian friends, take a good hard look at Jesus.... He's the centerpiece of everything we believe, faithful in everything God gave him to do.

Hebrews 3:1,2 THE MESSAGE

· **Advent Wreath:** Each Advent Sunday, light one of three purple candles in an evergreen wreath.

On Christmas Eve, light a white candle (the Christ candle) and place it in the center to commemorate His birth and recognize Him as the Light of the World, who dwells in our hearts (John 8:12).

· **Nativity Advent Calendar:** Each December morning, family members add a figure to the Nativity scene. The story of Jesus is slowly revealed as the season unfolds and the story is complete when the Christ Child is added on Christmas Eve.

· **Candy Advent Tree:** Drill 24 holes in a tree-shaped block of wood. Stick green and red tootsie or bubblegum pops in each hole. On each day of Advent, the first to show genuine Christmas kindness is given the lollipop.

Remember His marvelous works which He has done, His wonders....
1 Chronicles 16:12 NKJV

29

Angels & Advent

Christmas plays and pageants are popular in Poland, where the Christmas story is recited in verse and acted out by marionettes. Polish boys in costumes go from house to house carrying Christmas cribs and singing carols.

It is a Polish custom not to serve Christmas dinner until the evening star has appeared. A vacant chair is always placed at the table to signify that a place has been made for the Little Child of Bethlehem.

When they saw the star, they rejoiced exceedingly with great joy.
Matthew 2:10 NASB

A thrill of hope the weary world rejoices,

For yonder breaks a new and glorious morn.

Fall on your knees,

Oh, hear the angel voices.

O night divine,

O night when Christ was born!

O night, O holy night,

O night divine.

— Adolph Adam

Come, kneel before the Lord our Maker, for he is our God.
Psalm 95:6,7 TLB

Angels & Advent

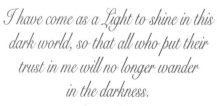

In Bethlehem, at the Church of the Nativity, at the base of the stairway lies a subterranean chamber or vault, 33 feet long and about 12 feet in width. The marble walls blaze with lamps, which burn continually, night and day. In the floor is a large silver star. Around it, a Latin inscription which, in English, reads: "Here Jesus Christ was born of the Virgin Mary."

I have come as a Light to shine in this dark world, so that all who put their trust in me will no longer wander in the darkness.

John 12:46 TLB

32

This is the place where God first became "manifest in the flesh." What rejoicing it brings to think that we, also, can sing a joyful Christmas hymn in the very town over which hung the Star of Bethlehem, and, "approximately, on the spot where the Virgin Mary brought forth her first-born Son," while the air above was vocal with the music of the angels.

—T. L. Cuyler

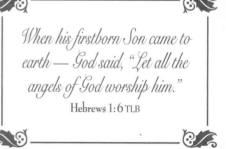

When his firstborn Son came to earth — God said, "Let all the angels of God worship him."
Hebrews 1:6 TLB

Angels & Advent

How a life leaves this world we know not, except that the heart of flesh left behind ceases to beat. How a life enters this world we know not, except that the heart nourished by the mother's heart begins its own beating.

Let the curtains fall.

Leave the wise Elizabeth and her own sleeping babe, alone with the pure Mary and her Son Jesus coming into the world to save sinners.

It is Holy Night.

— Henry Van Dyke

Mary quietly treasured these things in her heart and often thought about them.

Luke 2:19 TLB

The First Christmas...
the Birth of Jesus

Joseph went from the Galilean town of Nazareth up to Bethlehem in Judah, David's town, for the census. As a descendant of David, he had to go there. He went with Mary, his fiancée, who was pregnant. While they were there, the time came for her to give birth. She gave birth to a son, her firstborn. She wrapped him in a blanket and laid him in a manger, because there was no room in the hostel.

— Luke 2:4-7 THE MESSAGE

The First Christmas...
the Birth of Jesus

One of the most cherished traditions of Naples is that of the sixteenth-century lullaby sung in San Domenico's Church on Christmas Eve and during the Christmas novena.

On Christmas Eve, a crowd gathers on the piazza outside the church to reenact the Advent of Christ. From within the church appear a cross-bearer and acolytes and one of the Dominican Fathers.

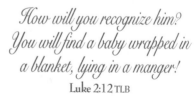

How will you recognize him?
You will find a baby wrapped in
a blanket, lying in a manger!
Luke 2:12 TLB

Presently a woman comes forward and reverently places the figure of a child in the hands of the priest. A procession is formed and the "Bambino," as it is called, is carried in and laid in its place in the crib.

All present kneel in adoration while violins softly play, filling the basilica with the strains of the ancient lullaby, "Dormi, Benigne Jesu, in dulci somno." The crowd, moved to tender devotion by the mystery of the Nativity, then takes up the sweet melody.

> *They came into the house and saw the Child with Mary His mother; and they fell down and worshiped Him.*
>
> Matthew 2:11 NASB

37

The First Christmas... the Birth of Jesus

A touchingly beautiful Christmas custom is observed at early Mass on Christmas morning in some parts of South America. As the Nativity is reenacted, an Indian lullaby is sung to quiet the Christ Child in His cradle of straw. The music of little bells and rattles can be heard as worshippers celebrate the Divine Birth.

I will lie down in peace and sleep, for though I am alone, O Lord, you will keep me safe.
Psalm 4:8 TLB

Born in a stable,

Cradled in a manger,

In the world His hands had made,

Born a stranger.

— Christina Georgina
Rossetti

*Before anything else existed,
there was Christ, with God.*

John 1:1 TLB

39

The First Christmas...
the Birth of Jesus

On Christmas Day in the year 1492, Christopher Columbus officially established his first American settlement on the northern coast of the island of San Domingo. At eleven o'clock on Christmas Eve, the Santa Maria was riding almost motionless on a calm sea when suddenly it struck a sand bar.

May the Lord of peace himself give you his peace no matter what happens.
2 Thessalonians 3:16 TLB

40

Early on Christmas morning the chief of an Indian tribe, a league and a half away, heard of the wreck. He sent canoes and men, who spent a long day helping the sailors salvage what they could from their damaged vessel.

As a memorial of gratitude for the rescue of the ship's crew and in honor of the Feast of the Nativity, Columbus named the fortress and adjacent village "La Navidad" the Spanish equivalent for "The Nativity."

Give to the Lord the glory due His name.

1 Chronicles 16:29 NKJV

41

The First Christmas...
the Birth of Jesus

It was the day before Christmas in 1818. In the little village of Oberndorf, something had gone wrong with the church organ. It appeared that mice had been chewing at the bellows and the organ would not make a sound.

Father Joseph Mohr, pastor of the little church worried that there would be no music for the Midnight Mass.

The peace I give isn't fragile like the peace the world gives.
John 14:27 TLB

Then the good priest had an inspiration. He would write a new Christmas song and have Franz Gruber compose a simple melody suited to guitar and mandolin. Gruber worked feverishly on the score, leaving time for only a brief rehearsal. That night at Midnight Mass, the new Christmas song was heard for the first time.

In the more than 100 years that have passed since its composition, "Silent Night, Holy Night!" has been sung throughout the world. What joyous peace continues to flood our hearts when we hear those beautiful words.

The Lord gives strength to his people; the Lord blesses his people with peace.
Psalm 29:11 NIV

43

The First Christmas... the Birth of Jesus

Silent night, holy night!

All is calm, all is bright

Round yon Virgin Mother and Child,

Holy Infant so tender
and mild!

Sleep in heavenly
peace,

Sleep in heavenly
peace.

— Joseph Mohr
& Franz Gruber

*"Behold, the virgin shall be
with child, and shall bear a Son, and
they shall call His name Immanuel,"
which translated means, "God with us."*

Matthew 1:23 NASB

In the Ukraine, singers go about the villages carrying a manger and singing folk songs, which tell of the birth of Christ.

The shepherds told everyone what had happened and what the angel had said to them about this child.

Luke 2:17 TLB

45

The First Christmas... the Birth of Jesus

In India at Christmas in the sweet
and chilly dawn,

We wake to hear the singing, "Lo! Christ
the Lord is born."

"Oh, come, let us
adore Him,"

Our Indian
children sing,

"Oh, come, and
let us worship,

The little baby King."

*The good man walks along in the ever-
brightening light of God's favor; the
dawn gives way to morning splendor.*

Proverbs 4:18 TLB

So over here in India we keep His birthday too,

Just as all His dear children in other countries do.

We have our glorious sunshine; we have our waving palms;

We have the Babe of Mary,
the carols, and the psalms.

— Minnie Moses Narasaravupet

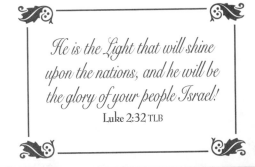

He is the Light that will shine upon the nations, and he will be the glory of your people Israel!
Luke 2:32 TLB

47

The First Christmas...
the Birth of Jesus

According to authorities the stable where Jesus was born was 32 feet 9¾ inches in length and 13 feet 1½ inches in width. The manger He was placed into was 2 feet 6 inches in length and 1 foot 6¾ inches in width.

And His name will be called Wonderful, Counselor, Mighty God, Everlasting Father, Prince of Peace.

Isaiah 9:6 NKJV

Oh come little children from cot and from hall,

Oh come to the manger, in Bethlehem's stall,

There meekly He lieth,
   the heavenly Child,

So poor and so humble, so
   sweet and so mild.

*Bethlehem...out of you will come
a ruler who will be the shepherd
of my people Israel.*
Matthew 2:6 NIV

49

The First Christmas...
the Birth of Jesus

A line in history was drawn on the first Christmas Day...

The Palace and the Stable

It was the 753rd year since the founding of Rome and Gaius Julius Caesar Octavianus Augustus was living in the palace of the Palatine Hill, busily engaged in the task of ruling his empire.

God...enforces peace in heaven.
Job 25:2 TLB

In a little village of distant Syria, Mary, the wife of Joseph the Carpenter, was tending her little boy, born in a stable of Bethlehem.

This is a strange world.

Before long, the palace and the stable were to meet in open combat.

And the stable was to emerge victorious.

— Hendrik Willem Van Loon

He will reign over the house of Jacob forever; and His kingdom will have no end.

Luke 1:33 NASB

51

The First Christmas...
the Birth of Jesus

Angels and archangels
    May have gathered there.
Cherubim and seraphim
    Thronged the air:
But only
    His Mother,
In her
    maiden bliss,
Worshipped
    the Beloved
With a kiss.
— Christina
    Georgina
    Rossetti

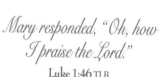

Mary responded, "Oh, how I praise the Lord."
Luke 1:46 TLB

One of the most potent, though silent testimonials of Christ, is the fact that all chronology is dated "before" or "after" Christ. B.C. and A.D. meet and part at His crib.

> Therefore the Lord Himself will give you a sign: Behold, a virgin will be with child and bear a son, and she will call His name Immanuel.
>
> Isaiah 7:14 NASB

53

The First Christmas...
the Birth of Jesus

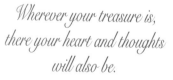

The earth has grown old with its burden of care,

But at Christmas it always is young,

The heart of the jewel burns lustrous and fair,

And its soul full of music bursts forth on the air,

When the song of the angels is sung.

— Phillips Brooks

Wherever your treasure is, there your heart and thoughts will also be.

Luke 12:34 TLB

First Eyewitnesses...

As the angel choir withdrew into heaven, the sheepherders talked it over. "Let's get over to Bethlehem as fast as we can and see for ourselves what God has revealed to us." They left, running, and found Mary and Joseph, and the baby lying in the manger.

— Luke 2:15,16 THE MESSAGE

First Eyewitnesses...

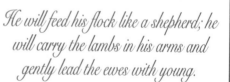

The first Noel the angel did say

Was to certain poor shepherds in fields as they lay;

In fields where they lay, keeping their sheep,

On a cold winter's night that was so deep.

Noel, Noel,

Noel, Noel,

Born is the King of Israel.

He will feed his flock like a shepherd; he will carry the lambs in his arms and gently lead the ewes with young.

Isaiah 40:11 TLB

In Egypt, Christians burn candles, lamps and logs in great numbers on the Eve of Christmas, as symbols of the "Shepherds' Fire."

For You will light my lamp; The LORD my God will enlighten my darkness.
Psalm 18:28 NKJV

57

First Eyewitnesses...

According to legend, when the shepherds came to Bethlehem, they found the Holy Family suffering from the cold. The youngest shepherd went out and gathered a bundle of ash sticks to kindle a fire, and even though the wood was green, the fire immediately burned brightly and freely.

Let the mountains and hills, the fruit trees and cedars...all praise the Lord together.

Psalm 148:9, 13 TLB

By the light and warmth of this blaze, the newborn Babe was washed and swaddled. Throughout the ages, when the sap of all other woods prevents their kindling, the ash retains its generous power — the more freshly it has been cut, the more brightly it will burn.

The true Light arrived to shine on everyone coming into the world.

1 John 1:9 TLB

First Eyewitnesses...

Banbury Tarts for Christmas

½ c. Raisins

½ c. Currants

4 Figs, Cut Fine

4 Tbsp. Orange Juice

1 c. Sugar

2 tsp. Water

½ c. Chopped Walnuts

Cook first ingredients 20 minutes; add walnuts and orange juice, cooking 20 minutes. Mix pastry dough: 3 c. Flour, ¾ c. Crisco, 1 tsp. Salt and Ice Water. Make 3-in. squares of pastry; fill mixture; fold to make tarts. Bake 45 min. at 350°. Makes 20-25.

Man does not live on bread alone but on every word that comes from the mouth of the LORD.

Deuteronomy 8:3 NIV

60

Plum Pudding and Mince Pie

Originally called "Christmas pudding" and "Christmas pie," the mixture of spices represent the offerings brought to the Infant Christ by the Wise Men.

The "Christmas pie" was made in the shape of a cradle in which Jesus was laid. To represent the manger, strips of pastry were sometimes laid crosswise over the pie.

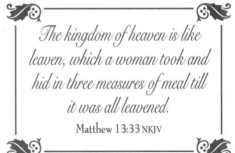

The kingdom of heaven is like leaven, which a woman took and hid in three measures of meal till it was all leavened.

Matthew 13:33 NKJV

61

First Eyewitnesses...

W ell-to-do families in Serbia keep open house for three days at Christmas and all comers, friends or enemies, strangers or beggars, are welcome to come to the table.

On Christmas Eve, the Serbians have a saying, "Tonight Earth is blended with Paradise."

When you put on a dinner...invite the poor, the crippled, the lame, and the blind...God will reward you for inviting those who can't repay you.
Luke 14:12-14 TLB

According to an ancient folk story, the scant fire that had been built to keep the Christ Child warm as He lay in His manger slowly began to die out.

Seeing this, a little robin hopped up to the fire and began flapping its wings in an effort to fan the embers back to life. As it fanned, the breast feathers of the little bird radiated the glow of the fire and became red. They remain so to this day.

Even the sparrows and swallows are welcome to come and nest among your altars and there have their young.
Psalm 84:3 TLB

63

First Eyewitnesses...

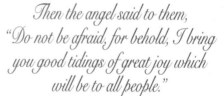

At early dawn on Christmas in the court of the church, Assyrians make a small fire called the fire of the Shepherds. This is then carried through the church. It represents the fire by which the shepherds were watching their flock.

When a baby is born, Assyrians celebrate the birth by inviting their neighbors to come in and eat sweet meats and fruit.

In light of this custom, the priest gives a walnut or piece of fruit to each of the faithful on Christmas. This is done in celebration of the birth of Christ. These are called *Bizqu d' Maran* ("Our Lord's Pebbles").

Then the angel said to them, "Do not be afraid, for behold, I bring you good tidings of great joy which will be to all people."

Luke 2:10 NKJV

Those shepherds thro' the lonely night
Sat watching by their sheep,
Until they saw the heav'nly host
Who neither tire nor sleep,
All singing Glory, glory,
In festival they keep.
— Christina Georgina
  Rossetti

Suddenly an angel appeared among them, and the landscape shone bright with the glory of the Lord.

Luke 2:9 TLB

First Eyewitnesses...

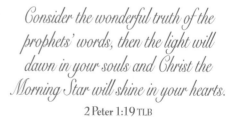

One Christmas Eve, by torchlight, Brother Francis read aloud the story of the birth of Jesus. As the townspeople gathered, he read to them of the shepherds and the angels' song.

He then spoke to them as a father might speak to his own children, telling them of love that is as gentle as a little child and willing to be poor and humble, as was the Baby who lay in a manger among the cattle.

Consider the wonderful truth of the prophets' words, then the light will dawn in your souls and Christ the Morning Star will shine in your hearts.

2 Peter 1:19 TLB

Saint Francis begged his listeners to put anger and hatred and envy out of their hearts and think only thoughts of peace and good will.

All listened eagerly while Brother Francis spoke, but the moment he finished, the great crowd broke into singing. Never before had such glorious hymns nor such joyous shouting been heard in the town of Greccio.

Only the mothers with babes in their arms and the shepherds in their woolly coats looked on silently and thought: "We are in Bethlehem."

> *Then the shepherds went back again to their fields and flocks, praising God for the visit of the angels, and because they had seen the child, just as the angel had told them.*
>
> Luke 2:20 TLB

67

First Eyewitnesses...

When we think of spices at Christmas, we often think of the wise men's gifts to Jesus. Potpourri and sachets are still a treasured gift.

ROSE SACHET

4 oz. Rose Petals

1 oz. Whole Rose Buds

½ oz. Whole Cloves

½ oz. Orris-Root Powder

2 drops Damask Rose Oil

Yes, there will be an abundance of flowers and singing and joy! The deserts will become as green as the Lebanon mountains.

Isaiah 35:2 TLB

* * * * * * * * * * * * * * * * * *

While shepherds watched their flocks by night,

All seated on the ground,

The angel of the Lord came down,

And glory shone around.

— Nahum Tate

*All who heard the shepherds'
story expressed astonishment.*
Luke 2:18 TLB

* * * * * * * * * * * * * * * * * *

First Eyewitnesses...

It came upon the midnight clear,
That glorious song of old,
From angels bending near the earth
To touch their harps of gold:
Peace on the earth,
goodwill to men
From heaven's all-
gracious King!"
The world in solemn
stillness lay
To hear the angels sing.
— Edmund H. Sears
1846

May all who are godly be happy in the Lord and crown him, our holy God.

Psalm 97:12 TLB

Everywhere, everywhere Christmas tonight!

For the Christ Child who comes is the master of all;

No Palace too great —

no cottage too small.

— Phillips Brooks

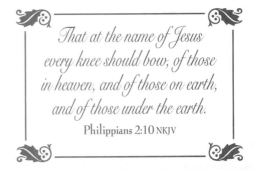

That at the name of Jesus every knee should bow, of those in heaven, and of those on earth, and of those under the earth.

Philippians 2:10 NKJV

It's a story tried and true
That began when the earth was new.
A mystery woven through the ages to save us.
Revealed — to celebrate His birth at Christmas.
So come; rejoice and sing.
Of our wonderful prophet, priest and king!
Oh, how we love to tell it again and again.
Of the baby Jesus, God's gift to man.

— Josanne Moore

A Star Lights the Way

After Jesus was born in Bethlehem village, Judah territory — this was during Herod's kingship — a band of scholars arrived in Jerusalem from the East. They asked around, "Where can we find and pay homage to the newborn King of the Jews? We observed a star in the eastern sky that signaled his birth. We're on pilgrimage to worship him."

— Matthew 2:1,2 THE MESSAGE

A Star Lights the Way

Rise, happy morn, rise, holy morn,

Draw forth the cheerful day from night;

O Father, touch the East, and light

The light that
shone when Hope
was born.

—Tennyson

*The Light from heaven
came into the world.*
John 3:19 TLB

Out from many a humble farmhouse, which had only a calico curtain in the window and a rag-carpet on the floor, has graduated the noblest manhood that has ruled in Church and State, or gone on foreign missions to the heathen world. Abraham Lincoln said that he owed all that was best in him to his loving mother; the candle that shone so brightly in the Kentucky log-cabin shed its light over our land and over the world....

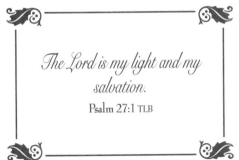

The Lord is my light and my salvation.
Psalm 27:1 TLB

75

A Star Lights the Way

When husband and wife make common cause in enthroning the Christmas Christ over their household, and in barring out the enemies that threaten the peace or the purity of their home, domestic life becomes as sweet as a song and as holy as a sacrament. In such a home the Christmas candles burn all the year round, and "the church in the house" becomes the beautiful preparation for and the prelude to the great family circle in the realms of glory.

—T. L. Cuyler

Take delight in honoring each other.
Romans 12:10 TLB

* * * * * * * * * * * * * * * * * * * *

The stars shone bright that Christmas night,

When Jesus lay on His bed of hay.

The shepherds came from far away

To find the place where the baby lay.

The wise men brought their
   gifts of love;

Led by the star that shone
   from above.

— E. Webster

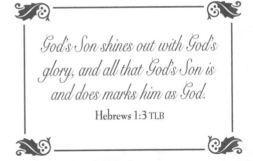

God's Son shines out with God's glory, and all that God's Son is and does marks him as God.

Hebrews 1:3 TLB

* * * * * * * * * * * * * * * * * * *

A Star Lights the Way

What star is this, with beams so bright,
Which shames the sun's less radiant light?
It shines to announce a newborn King, —
Glad tidings of our
God to bring.

— Translated from
the Latin, by
Rev. J. Chandler
*Hymns of the
Primitive Church*

*God is so glorious that even the moon
and stars are less than nothing as
compared to him.*
Job 25:5 TLB

In Austria, great preparations are made for the Christmas festival. Two huge loaves of bread are baked, which are meant to represent the Old and New Testaments.

On Christmas Eve, the family lights one of three special candles and the family sings a hymn. Before they begin to eat, the father takes the candle in his hand and says, "Christ is born." Then each child in turn takes the taper and standing on a stool repeats three times, "Praised be the Lord! Christ is born."

On Christmas Day, the family lights the second candle, and on New Year's Day, the third candle is lit, ending the Christmas festivities.

Your word is a lamp to my feet and a light for my path.
Psalm 119:105 NIV

79

A Star Lights the Way

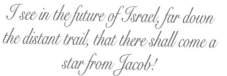

It was the eve of Christmas; the snow lay deep and white.
I sat beside my window and looked into the night.
I heard the church bells ringing, I saw the bright stars shine,
And childhood came again to me with all its dreams divine.
Then as I listened to the bells and watched the skies afar,

Out of the east majestic
there rose one radiant star,

And every other star
grew pale before that
heavenly glow.

It seemed to bid me
follow, and I could not
choose but go.

—Frederic E. Weatherly

*I see in the future of Israel, far down
the distant trail, that there shall come a
star from Jacob!*
Numbers 24:17 TLB

Alaskans have a Christmas custom they call, "Going round with the star."

A star-shaped wooden frame is covered with bright tissue paper and for three nights, youngsters carry it from door to door. Wherever they stop to sing carols, the children are invited into the house and given gifts.

On the third night, the children attend a party, where they wear masks to represent Herod's soldiers. They try to capture the star and destroy it, just as Herod's men tried to destroy the Infant Christ.

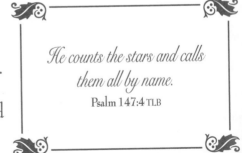

He counts the stars and calls them all by name.
Psalm 147:4 TLB

81

A Star Lights the Way

According to an ancient folktale, a forester and his household locked their door and gathered around a cheerful fire one stormy Christmas Eve. By and by knocking was heard outside. The father of the house opened the door to find a little child, cold, hungry, and all but exhausted.

The family kindly welcomed, warmed, and fed the child. One of the children insisted on giving up his bed to the stranger.

He who has a generous eye will be blessed, for he gives of his bread to the poor.
Proverbs 22:9 NKJV

In the morning, the family was aroused by the singing of a choir of angels; and looking at their unbidden guest, they saw Him transfigured, for He was none other than the Christ Child.

He broke off a branch from a fir tree, and set it in the earth. "See," He said, "I have gladly received your gifts, and this is my gift to you. Henceforward, this tree shall always bear its fruit at Christmas, and you shall always have abundance."

There can be no need to elaborate the meaning of this tale. Remember who it was that said, "Inasmuch as ye have done it to one of the least of these, ye did it unto me."

Love each other just as much as I love you.
John 13:34 TLB

A Star Lights the Way

According to an ancient folktale, when Christ was born, an olive tree, a date palm, and a fir tree stood about the manger. To honor the newborn King, the olive gave its fruit and the palm its dates as an offering, but the fir tree had nothing to give.

Observing this from their lofty perch, a number of stars gently descended from the heavens and rested on the boughs of the fir tree.

The folktale states that this was the origin of the first Christmas tree.

Let the trees of the forest rustle with praise.
Psalm 96:12 TLB

84

O Evergreen, O Evergreen, Thy garb unfading showeth,

O Evergreen, O Evergreen, Thy garb unfading showeth,

The flow'r of joy about my door,

Good cheer that faileth never more,

O Evergreen, O Evergreen,

My heart thy lesson knoweth.

— A German Folk Song

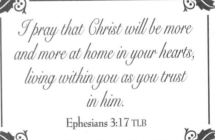

I pray that Christ will be more and more at home in your hearts, living within you as you trust in him.

Ephesians 3:17 TLB

A Star Lights the Way

This old, sobbing world of ours is one year older than it was when the last Christmas carol was chanted. It has had another 12 months of experiments and experiences; of advancement on many lines of human research, scientific discovery and acquisition. But it has not outgrown Jesus Christ. For Him it has discovered no substitute. The Star of Bethlehem is the only star that never sets.

—T.L. Cuyler

Of the increase of His government and peace there will be no end.
Isaiah 9:7 NKJV

Christmas Star Sugar Cookies

1 Pound Butter
5 c. Flour
Pinch of Salt
1 Tbsp. Vanilla

2 Eggs
2 c. Sugar
1 tsp. Baking Soda Dissolved in
3 Tbsp. Milk

Mix all ingredients in bowl with hands. Form into a ball, dust with flour, and chill thoroughly. When chilled, break into pieces and roll out as thin as possible. Dust with sugar and nutmeg, and cut with "star" cookie cutters. Bake at 350° for 12 minutes — just lightly browned. Can be decorated.

Makes 5-6 dozen.

Man did eat the bread of angels;
He sent them food in abundance.
Psalm 78:25 NASB

A Star Lights the Way

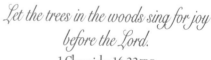

According to an ancient folktale, St. Boniface (St. Winifred) was preaching Christianity to the people of Germany one Christmas Eve, when he came upon a group of people standing around a huge oak tree. He was horrified to see that the group was preparing to offer a human sacrifice according to the Druid rites of the pagans.

In anger St. Boniface bravely hewed down the oak tree, and as it fell, a tall, young fir tree appeared in its place. Seeing this, he said to

Let the trees in the woods sing for joy before the Lord.
1 Chronicles 16:33 TLB

the people, "This new tree is unstained by blood. See how it points to the sky? You are to call it the tree of the Christ Child. Take it up and carry it into the castle of your chief."

"No longer shall you observe your secret and wicked rites in the shadow of the forest, but you shall hold ceremonies in your own homes that speak the message of peace and goodwill to all."

"A day is coming when every home in the land will celebrate the birthday of Christ by gathering around a fir tree in memory of this day and to the glory of God."

Come before him clothed in sacred garments.
Psalm 29:2 TLB

A Star Lights the Way

Three Kings came riding from far away,
Melchior, and Gaspar and Balthasar;
Three Wise Men out of the East were they,

And they traveled
by night and they
slept by day.

For their guide
was a beautiful,
wonderful star.

— Henry Wadsworth
Longfellow

I am...the bright and Morning Star.
Revelation 22:16 NKJV

The stars in the bright sky

Look'd down where He lay,

The little Lord Jesus

Asleep on the hay.

— Martin Luther

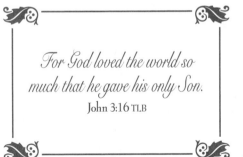

For God loved the world so much that he gave his only Son.
John 3:16 TLB

A Star Lights the Way

In Ireland, candles are placed in the windows on Christmas Eve. They are intended to serve as a guide and an invitation to all who, like Mary and Joseph on the first Christmas Eve, may be wandering about unable to find quarters for the night.

On this special night, poor wanderers and tramps are welcomed everywhere. They are given a good meal, a place to sleep, and sent on their way in the morning with a bit of money in their pockets.

Don't forget to be kind to strangers, for some who have done this have entertained angels without realizing it!
Hebrews 13:2 TLB

On Christmas Eve a Candlelight

To shine abroad through Christmas night,

That those who pass

may see its glow,

And walk with Christ

a mile or so.

> *Those who are wise shall shine like the brightness of the firmament, and those who turn many to righteousness like the stars forever and ever.*
>
> Daniel 12:3 NKJV

93

A Star Lights the Way

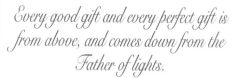

Christmas Tree Candles

According to an ancient folktale, a man was lost in a great woods. For days he wandered through the woods trying to find his way, but he always found himself back at the place where he started.

Finally, he was so exhausted that he thought he would surely die.

As night came on, the man saw that it was one of those beautiful blue nights when the heavens are filled with bright stars. By the light of the stars, he was able to find his way.

Every good gift and every perfect gift is from above, and comes down from the Father of lights.
James 1:17 NKJV

When he reached his home, the man found that it was Christmas Eve. The light of the Christmas stars had brought him home to his wife and children.

In thanksgiving, the man went back to the woods and cut down a small tree. Upon his return, he and his family covered the tree with little lighted candles.

Like the stars in the Christmas sky, the candles burned brightly in honor of the birthday of the Christ Child.

Let the countryside and everything in it rejoice!

1 Chronicles 16:32 TLB

A Star Lights the Way

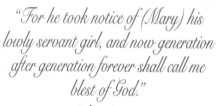

According to Irish tradition, only those bearing the name Mary are permitted to snuff the Christmas candle on Christmas Eve.

> *"For he took notice of (Mary) his lowly servant girl, and now generation after generation forever shall call me blest of God."*
> Luke 1:48 TLB

It was once a custom on the Twelfth Night of Christmas to place 12 candles in a circle inside a sieve of oats. A larger candle was placed in the center of the sieve. The candles were then lit and the sieve was placed as high as possible in the room.

This was done to demonstrate that the Savior and His Apostles serve as the lights of the world.

We have seen and testify that the Father has sent the Son as Savior of the world.
1 John 4:14 NKJV

A Star Lights the Way

According to tradition, *Mistletoe*, when used at Christmas, has romantic significance.

A spray is cunningly hung over a doorway or place of vantage beneath which the romantic "Mistletoe Kiss" may be claimed. A berry is plucked after each kiss. When the berries are gone, the privilege of kissing ceases.

Greet one another with a holy kiss.
Romans 16:16 NKJV

When Mary Lay Fretting

When Mary lay thinking that night in the hay

What little thing she would give Jesus for play,

His Father in Heaven hung out for a toy

The Star, and young Jesus
He carolled for joy.

— Peter Warlock (from "The
Five Lesser Joys of Mary")

*My hand has made both earth
and skies, and they are mine.*
Isaiah 66:2 TLB

A Star Lights the Way

W hether put in a drawer, on a shelf, or in a small decorative pillow, the fragrance of *rosemary* at Christmastime can provide a delightful welcome to any room.

PILLOW POTPOURRI

1 oz. *Hops*
1 oz. *Rosemary*
1 oz. Lemon *Verbena* Leaves
1 drop Lemon *Verbena* Oil

Mary took a jar of costly perfume...and the house was filled with fragrance.
John 12:3 TLB

Rosemary was once considered a Christmas green, along with *holly*, *mistletoe*, and *ivy*. It was admired for its fragrance rather than its color.

According to an ancient folktale, *rosemary* acquired its fragrance when Mary hung the swaddling clothes worn by the Christ Child on a *rosemary* bush to dry.

According to Spanish folktale, the bloom of the *rosemary* plant was originally white. During the flight into Egypt, the Holy Family stopped to rest and Mary laid her purple mantle over a *rosemary* bush. It is said, that the flowers changed from white to deep lavender in her honor.

Even the wilderness and desert will rejoice in those days; the desert will blossom with flowers.

Isaiah 35:1 TLB

A Star Lights the Way

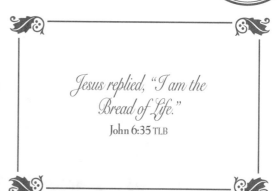

In France, tradition includes a gigantic wicker figure called "Melchior," after one of the three Magi. Clothed in a fantastic garb and with a huge basket strapped to his back, Melchior is mounted upon a donkey and taken from door to door to gather whatever the generous may give, including figs, almonds, bread, cheese, olives, sausages, and the like.

Jesus replied, "I am the Bread of Life."
John 6:35 TLB

When "Melchior" has finished his round, the basket is emptied onto a table at the church door, and the poor of the parish are invited to come and receive portions of the good things.

In the meantime the church bells ring, and a torch blazes beside the table, representing the "Star" that guided Melchior to Bethlehem.

And if you...men know how to give good gifts to your children, won't your Father in heaven even more certainly give good gifts to those who ask him for them?

Matthew 7:11 TLB

103

A Star Lights the Way

The Christ Child stood at Mary's knee,

His hair was like a crown,

And all the flowers

looked up at Him,

And all the stars

looked down.

— G. K. Chesterton

Heaven is My throne, and the earth is My footstool.
Isaiah 66:1 NKJV

O morning stars, together
Proclaim the holy birth,
And praises sing to God the King,
And peace to men
on earth.
— Phillips Brooks

Let the heavens be glad, the earth rejoice....It is the Lord who reigns.
1 Chronicles 16:31 TLB

A Star Lights the Way

Dating back to Byzantine times, it is the custom of children in the Greek Empire to celebrate their "Feast of Lights" by going around on Christmas morning and collecting walnuts, figs, raisins, and sweets. This is known as "Luck [or favor] of Christ."

His light shines down on all the earth.
Job 25:3 TLB

Magi Bring Gifts

Herod then arranged a secret meeting with the scholars from the East. Pretending to be as devout as they were, he got them to tell him exactly when the birth-announcement star appeared. Then he told them the prophecy about Bethlehem, and said, "Go find this child. Leave no stone unturned. As soon as you find him, send word and I'll join you at once in your worship.

Instructed by the king, they set off. Then the star appeared again, the same star they had seen in the eastern skies. It led them on until it hovered over the place of the child.

— Matthew 2:7-9 THE MESSAGE

Magi Bring Gifts

Visitors from Afar

Down the narrow street swayed three tall, richly harnessed camels carrying three strangers in costly raiment. They halted in front of the house of Lemuel and dismounted.

They were wise men of the East, Magians from the mountains of Persia. They said that a sign in the sky had led them to do homage to a heavenly King whose coming was foretold by the books of Zoroaster, as well as by the Jewish prophets.

Majesty and honor march before him, strength and gladness walk beside him.
1 Chronicles 16:27 TLB

So they let down their corded bales and brought out gifts of gold and frankincense and myrrh. Kneeling in the house, they presented their tribute to the child Jesus.

Whether or not the infant Jesus knew anything of this visit by the Magi, except perhaps the glitter of their gold and the sweet smell of their incense, who can tell? But doubtless his parents spoke to him about it in later years.

— *Even Unto Bethlehem,*

by Henry Van Dyke

Jesus of Nazareth, the King of the Jews.
John 19:19 NKJV

109

Magi Bring Gifts

The magi of the East, in sandals worn,
Knelt reverent, sweeping round,
With long pale beards, their gifts
upon the ground,
The incense,
myrrh, and gold.
— Elizabeth
    Barrett
    Browning

*His mercy goes on from generation to
generation, to all who reverence him.*
Luke 1:50 TLB

O come, all ye faithful,
Joyful and triumphant,
O come ye, O come ye to Bethlehem;
Come and behold Him,
Born the King of angels:
O come, let us adore Him,
O come, let us adore Him,
O come, let us adore Him,
Christ the Lord.

— Anonymous, Latin; Tr.
Frederick Oakeley

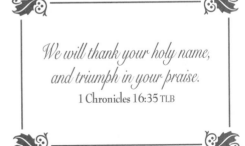

*We will thank your holy name,
and triumph in your praise.*
1 Chronicles 16:35 TLB

111

Magi Bring Gifts

In Russia, *Babuska* (grandmother) distributes the Christmas gifts.

According to a folktale, Babuska refused an opportunity to accompany the Three Kings on their journey and misdirected them when they asked how to find their way to Bethlehem.

According to another folktale, Babuska refused to take the Holy Family in when they were fleeing to Egypt. Regretting this, she goes about on Christmas Eve looking for the Christ Child and distributing gifts to all children.

Glory in His holy name; let the hearts of those rejoice who seek the Lord!

1 Chronicles 16:10 NKJV

In France, only the children receive gifts. In some parts of the country, a youth is dressed in white and wears a crown set around with many little wax candles. He is said to represent the Christ Child and carries a bell and a basket full of goodies.

Another person carrying a bunch of switches accompanies the youth. At the sight of him, naughty little boys and girls hide. The youth representing the Christ Child asks that they be forgiven. Once the children promise to behave better, they are given their gifts and shown the Christmas tree.

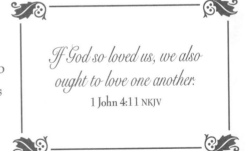

If God so loved us, we also ought to love one another.
1 John 4:11 NKJV

113

Magi Bring Gifts

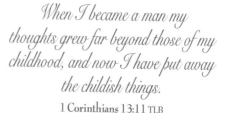

The Week Before Christmas

'Tis the week before Christmas and every night,
As soon as the children are snuggled up tight
And have sleepily murmured their wishes and prayers,
Such fun as goes on in the parlor downstairs!

For Father, Big Brother
and Grandfather too,
Start in with great vigor
their youth to renew.

The games are unwrapped
and directions are read
And they play till it's long
past their hour for bed.

*When I became a man my
thoughts grew far beyond those of my
childhood, and now I have put away
the childish things.*

1 Corinthians 13:11 TLB

114

They try to solve puzzles and each one enjoys
The magical thrill of mechanical toys.
Even mother must play with a doll that can talk,
And if you assist it, is able to walk.
It's really no matter if paint may be scratched,
Or a cog wheel, a nut, or a bolt gets detached;
The grown-ups are having great fun — all is well;
The children don't know it, and Santa won't tell.

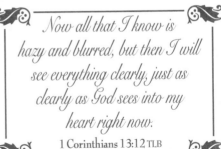

Now all that I know is hazy and blurred, but then I will see everything clearly, just as clearly as God sees into my heart right now.

1 Corinthians 13:12 TLB

Magi Bring Gifts

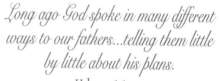

An Advent Calendar of German and Scandinavian origin is a special gift at Christmas. In December, the recipient opens one small window each day before Christmas. Behind each opening is a special picture, message, or story that progresses as the days go by.

To begin; draw, color or paint a picture on white heavy stock paper — a Christmas scene, such as a church, a crèche, a decorated tree, or a simple (winter) landscape with buildings.

Long ago God spoke in many different ways to our fathers...telling them little by little about his plans.

Hebrews 1:1 TLB

Upon completion of your picture, place it on a cutting board, and (using an X-ACTO knife or a single-edge razor blade) cut out each window on three sides, leaving one side as the hinge. Then lightly pencil an outline of each window opening onto a second sheet placed underneath. On the second sheet with 25 empty squares you can then draw, write, or paste pictures, messages or a story.

Glue sheets together at the edges, *carefully* lining up pictures and windows. Press flat with books for several hours, add glitter, or any finishing touches — a cherished keepsake for years to come!

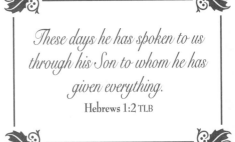

These days he has spoken to us through his Son to whom he has given everything.
Hebrews 1:2 TLB

Magi Bring Gifts

The first real Christmas cards appear to have been printed in London in 1846. Almost 1,000 copies were made — that would have been considered a very large sale at the time.

It was not until about 1860 that the custom of using cards to convey Christmas greetings became popular. The tradition has gained strength through the years, and today, Christmas cards are produced by the millions.

Now here is my greeting which I am writing with my own hand...May the blessing of our Lord Jesus Christ be upon you all.
2 Thessalonians 3:17,18 TLB

In Spain, children receive their gifts from the Wise Men, especially Balthasar.

The children place their shoes in rows by the doors and windows, where the Wise Men, repeating their pilgrimage each year, will see them and fill them with toys and good things.

The Christmas toy is the Child Jesus in the crib, made of painted clay. Instead of hanging up their stockings for gifts, their tradition is the *Nacimiento* — the hiding of shoes and slippers.

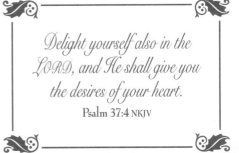

Delight yourself also in the LORD, and He shall give you the desires of your heart.
Psalm 37:4 NKJV

Magi Bring Gifts

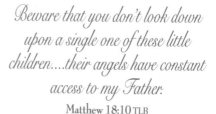

Alfie's Christmas Boots

According to a charming folktale, a small lad asked Jesus for a pair of boots. His own were terribly worn, and his mother, with no money to buy new ones, had been carrying him to and from school rather than let him walk through the damp streets. The lad seemed to be getting heavier every day.

One evening, the lad's mother broke down and cried because she was afraid she would no longer be able to carry him.

Alfie puckered up his forehead and looked grave.

Beware that you don't look down upon a single one of these little children....their angels have constant access to my Father.
Matthew 18:10 TLB

"I'll have to tell Jesus about it," he said. His mother, half-awed and half-amused, listened while he put the matter before his Friend, in plain, straightforward language.

"Dear Jesus," she heard him say, "You send other little boys shoes and things to wear: please send some to me."

After Alfie had eaten his supper and gone to bed, there was a knock at the door. A neighbor stood outside the door with a pair of boots, which were getting too small for her own son, but would do splendidly for Alfie.

Mother tiptoed back to Alfie's bedside, and because he was asleep, she laid the boots beside him on his pillow. His shout awakened her in the morning. "Mother! They've come!" he cried. "He knew my size, too. And there's no hole in the ceiling."

— Hugh Redwood (from "God in the Slums")

Oh, give thanks to the Lord!
1 Chronicles 16:8 NKJV

Magi Bring Gifts

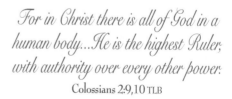

The gifts of the Magi were symbolic of their three-fold faith; the gold signified that He was King; the incense that He was God; and myrrh, that He was man and doomed to death.

According to legend, Caspar, the king of Tarsus, the land of merchants made the offering of gold. Melchior, the king of Arabia and Nubia, offered frankincense, and Balthasar, king of Saba, "the land of spices," offered myrrh.

For in Christ there is all of God in a human body...He is the highest Ruler, with authority over every other power.
Colossians 2:9,10 TLB

Long years ago
Wise men with joy
Brought birthday gifts
To a small boy.
— M. Lanning
Shane

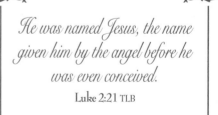

He was named Jesus, the name given him by the angel before he was even conceived.

Luke 2:21 TLB

Magi Bring Gifts

Christmas Crackers: Recycle wrapping or tissue scraps into exciting and easy-to-make table favors for the Christmas feast.

- Gather paper, glue, string, candy, or other goodies and a toilet tissue tube.

- Cut the toilet tissue tube in half; let the kids do the rest.

- Cut colored tissue and wrapping paper in rectangular shapes.

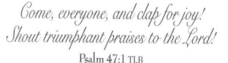

Come, everyone, and clap for joy!
Shout triumphant praises to the Lord!
Psalm 47:1 TLB

- Roll the toilet tissue tube up in both papers with the longer tissue paper to the inside, gluing or taping the seams of each paper.

- Fill the inside of the tube with an assortment of goodies. A firecracker "popping" string could be skillfully enclosed for excitement.

- Tie off the ends and clip the tissue ends to make it look like fringe.

- To open, pull both ends until it "pops!"

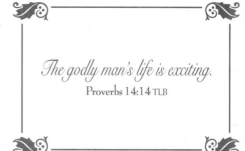

The godly man's life is exciting.
Proverbs 14:14 TLB

125

Magi Bring Gifts

Eight things are always associated with Christmas.

First and foremost is its religious significance. The other seven are: hanging the *mistletoe*, burning the Yule log, the Christmas tree, the Christmas carol, the greeting card, the Christmas stocking, and Santa Claus.

These eight have remained symbols of Christmas throughout the years.

Jesus Christ is the same yesterday, today, and forever.
Hebrews 13:8 TLB

In northern Germany, gifts are attributed to Knecht Ruprecht. He is represented as an old, bearded man covered with fur or straw. His name varies in different localities.

> *Therefore by Him let us continually offer the sacrifice of praise to God...giving thanks to His name.*
>
> Hebrews 13:15 NKJV

Magi Bring Gifts

In Germany, the Christ Child (*das Christkindlein* or *Christkind'l*) is the popular source of Christmas gifts. The folktale states that he appears on Christmas Eve and inquires how the children have behaved. After asking them to recite a prayer and sing a hymn, he distributes the gifts. Kris Kringle is a variation of *Christkind'l*.

All German children visit their godfather's home at Christmas and find a gift waiting for them.

Oh, give thanks to the Lord, for he is good; His love and his kindness go on forever.
1 Chronicles 16:34 TLB

128

It ain't the gift a feller gits, it ain't the shape ner size,
   that sets the heart to beatin' and puts sunshine in yer eyes.

It ain't the value of the thing, ner how it's wrapped ner tied;
   it's something else aside from this that makes you glad inside.

It's knowin' that it represents a love both deep an' true,
   that someone carries in his heart and
   wants to slip to you.

It's knowin' that some folks love you and tell
   you in this way — jest sorter actin' out
   the things they long to say.

So 'tain't the gift a feller gets, ner how it's
   wrapped ner tied, it's knowin' that folks
   like you, that makes you glad inside.

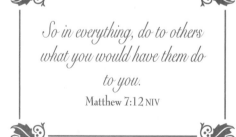

So in everything, do to others what you would have them do to you.
Matthew 7:12 NIV

Magi Bring Gifts

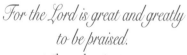

St. Nicholas is vested as a bishop in European countries. It seems it was right here in America that Santa was given his change of clothes and became a red-faced, bewhiskered gentleman of the jester type.

For the Lord is great and greatly to be praised.
1 Chronicles 16:25 NKJV

130

Legend has it that the popular custom of using stockings to hold gifts and goodies on Christmas originated one Christmas Eve when St. Nicholas dropped a purse of money down the chimney as a gift to a poor family. Instead of falling on the hearth, the purse rolled into a stocking on the floor nearby where it was found the next morning.

Let us stop just saying we love people; let us really love them, and show it by our actions.

1 John 3: 18 TLB

Magi Bring Gifts

In Puerto Rico, the children put boxes on the rooftops for Santa instead of hanging stockings inside.

A most picturesque and beautiful celebration known as "Bethlehem Day" is observed by the children on January 12, in memory of the coming of the Magi.

It consists of a procession through the streets led by three children, dressed as the Wise Men of the East. The children wear colorful costumes and ride on ponies or horses, holding the gifts for the Infant King in their hands. Behind the children dressed as Wise Men come those dressed as angels and shepherds. Flute players bring up the rear.

Declare His glory among the nations,
His wonders among all peoples.
1 Chronicles 16:24 NKJV

132

Create your own Magi gifts for those special loved ones with a sweet tooth. This candy is worth its weight in gold!

Toffee Treasures

1 c. Sugar
¼ c. Water
½ c. Chopped Pecans
1 (6-oz.) Pkg. Semi-Sweet
    Chocolate Chips

½ tsp. Salt
½ c. Butter

In saucepan, cook sugar, water, salt, and butter to light crack (285°). Add nuts, stir, and pour thinly onto Teflon cookie sheet. Pour chips on top, and spread with knife after melted. Sprinkle with nut pieces. Cool, break in pieces, and wrap. Makes about one pound.

He fills my life with good things!
Psalm 103:5 TLB

Magi Bring Gifts

One Christmas in the Life of St. Therese

Therese was now almost fourteen. Then came the memorable Christmas of 1886, when, in her own words, "There occurred a species of miracles that made me grow up in a moment."

On this Christmas morning, having returned from Midnight Mass at Buissonnets, France, little Therese saw in the space before the fireplace her shoes filled with gifts just as they had been every

For the Lord is watching his children, listening to their prayers.
1 Peter 3:12 TLB

Christmas since she was able to remember. Up to this time her father and sisters had continued to treat her like a baby, as was perhaps natural, since she was the youngest of the family.

As she climbed the stairs to go to her room, she heard her father say these words which went straight to her heart: "These Christmas surprises are too childish for a girl as big as Therese; I hope that this will be the last year for them."

Mastering her tears, she ran downstairs, picked up her gifts and, with the triumphant air of a queen, she placed them before her father. No longer could any trace of opposition be seen on his smiling face. "Charity entered my heart," records St. Therese, "together with the need of always forgetting myself, and from that time on I was happy."

Seek the Lord and His strength;
seek His face evermore!
1 Chronicles 16:11 NKJV

Magi Bring Gifts

O Star of wonder, Star of night,
Star with Royal Beauty bright,
Westward leading,
Still proceeding,
Guide us to Thy
perfect Light.
— John Henry
Hopkins, Jr.

God is light and in Him is no darkness at all.
1 John 1:5 NKJV

Christmas In Our Hearts

The Word became flesh and blood,
and moved into the neighborhood.
We saw the glory with our own eyes,
the one-of-a-kind glory,
like Father, like Son,
Generous inside and out,
true from start to finish.

— John 1:14 THE MESSAGE

Christmas In Our Hearts

Joy is simply love looking at its treasures.

A Christian's joy is in loving Christ and loving other people because Christ loves them; it is in doing good to others, and so having a Christmas perpetually.

It is in looking forward to that world of glory where we shall be like Him, and shall see Him as He is. "Where I am," is a sweet assurance, "ye shall be also." Jesus offers to fill our homes and our hearts with joy, if we will only let Him do it.

We love Him because He first loved us.

1 John 4:19 NKJV

We cannot create canary birds, but we can provide cages and food for them, and fill our dwellings with their music. Even so we cannot create the spiritual gifts and blessings which the Christmas Jesus offers; but they are ours if we provide heart room for them.

The birds of peace and praise and joy will fly in fast enough if we only set the doors and windows of our soul wide open for the Joy-Bringing Christ.

—T. L. Cuyler

I will praise You, O Lord my God, with all my heart.

Psalm 86:12 NKJV

Christmas In Our Hearts

Good Christian men, rejoice
With heart, and soul, and voice;
Now ye hear of endless bliss: Joy! Joy!
Jesus Christ was born for this!
He hath opened the
heav'nly door,
And man is blessed
ever more.
Christ was born for
this!
Christ was born for
this!

—J. M. Neale

For unto us a Child is born, unto us a Son is given.
Isaiah 9:6 NKJV

In Lithuania on Christmas Eve, a layer of hay is placed on the table under the cloth in memory of the night in Bethlehem, and an unconsecrated wafer symbolizing the love and harmony of the season is shared by all present.

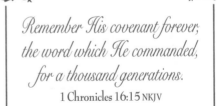

Remember His covenant forever,
the word which He commanded,
for a thousand generations.
1 Chronicles 16:15 NKJV

141

Christmas In Our Hearts

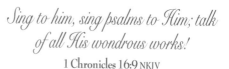

In Norway, instead of wishing the others a "Merry Christmas" the member of the household who wakes first sings a little hymn. Before retiring on Christmas Eve, the shoes of all the members of the household are placed in a row as a symbol that all will live peacefully together during the year.

Sing to him, sing psalms to Him; talk of all His wondrous works!

1 Chronicles 16:9 NKJV

Christian fellowship can warm the soul. Here's a Christmastime cider that can warm the body and whet the whistle of those story-tellers and carolers.

Mulled Cider

2 pints Cider
2 Apples
4 Cloves
¼ pint Water
1 Orange

2 oz. Brown Sugar
Cinnamon Stick
1 tsp. Ground Ginger

Bake the apples, stuck with 2 cloves each. Heat cider, but never boil. Separately, simmer gently (5 min.) the other ingredients (except orange) until sugar dissolves. Add to cider the baked apples, sliced orange and spiced water. Serve warm.

That I may come unto you with joy by the will of God, and may with you be refreshed.
Romans 15:32 NKJV

143

Christmas In Our Hearts

In "Even Unto Bethlehem" on the journey from the Jerusalem Temple to Bethlehem, Mary becomes overwhelmed with concern for her firstborn Son.

"We must take good care of Him, that is all," said Joseph. "He has been trusted to us. He cannot perish until His great task is done. God has promised. We are all in God's hand. We do not know how it will be worked out. We must do our part."

— Henry Van Dyke

He is the Lord our God.
1 Chronicles 16:14 NKJV

When people join the church they usually subscribe to some confession of faith; but about the most comprehensive one that any sincere convert can make may be condensed into these words: "I believe that it is Christ's business to save me and that it is my business to serve Christ."
—T. L. Cuyler

Give to the Lord, O families of the peoples, give to the Lord glory and strength.
1 Chronicles 16:28 NKJV

145

Christmas In Our Hearts

Always Christmas

Used to think that Christmas was nothin' but a date
Till I learned that truly you would never have to wait,
But that it's the spirit that never stays apart
If you let it find you, an' keep it in your heart.

Since I found that
Christmas is more
than just a day
Christmas came to
our house — an'
never went away!

— Wilbur D. Nesbit

*If we love one another, God abides
in us, and His love has been
perfected in us.*
1 John 4:12 NKJV

Our hearts they hold all Christmas dear,

And earth seems sweet and heaven seems near,

Oh, heaven was in His sight, I know,

That little Child

of long ago.

— Marjorie L. C. Pickthall

For Thou hast worked wonders, plans formed long ago, with perfect faithfulness.
Isaiah 25:1 NASB

147

Christmas In Our Hearts

According to an ancient folktale, a poor man, coming home from work one Christmas Eve found a little lost child. He was cold and crying. Pitying him, the poor man carried the child to his home where he showed his wife and family what he had found.

The poor man's family welcomed the child and gave him of their scanty meal, after which the children played with him like a brother.

He who loves his brother abides in the light.
1 John 2:10 NKJV

As the children were preparing for bed, the little stranger grew tall and a halo appeared round His head. "Bless us," said the mother, "it is the Lord Himself."

Immediately the vision vanished. Next morning, the family looked for some trace of the stranger and when they arrived at the place where the child was first seen, the ground was covered with flowers.

Praise the Lord, the God of Israel, for he has come to visit his people and has redeemed them.

Luke 1:68 TLB

Christmas In Our Hearts

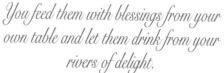

At Christmas be merry
and thank God of all,
And feast thy
poor neighbours,
the great with
the small.
— Thomas
   Tusser

You feed them with blessings from your own table and let them drink from your rivers of delight.
Psalm 36:8 TLB

In Denmark, where the tree has become as popular as in Germany, a pleasant custom is carried out.

Upon returning from church on Christmas Eve, the whole family, including servants and visitors, join hands and march round the Christmas tree singing carols.

Sing to the Lord, all the earth; proclaim the good news of His salvation from day to day.
1 Chronicles 16:23 NKJV

151

The Little Mud-Sparrows

(Jewish Legend)

How the little Jewish children
Upon a summer day,
Went down across the meadows
With the Child Christ to play.
And in the gold-green valley,
Where low the reed-grass lay,
They made them mock
mud-sparrows
Out of the meadow clay.
So, when these all were
fashioned,
and ranged in rows about,
"Now," said the little Jesus,
"We'll let the birds fly out."

*You are of more value than
many sparrows.*
Luke 12:7 NKJV

But earthen were the sparrows,
And earth they did remain,
Though loud the Jewish children
Cried out, and cried again.
Softly He leaned and whispered:
"Fly up to Heaven! Fly!"
And swift, His little sparrow
Went soaring to the sky.
Our souls are like the sparrows
Imprisoned in the clay,
Bless Him who came to give them wings
Upon a Christmas Day!

— Elizabeth Stuart Phelps

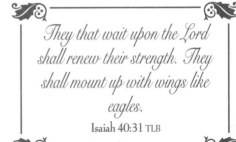

They that wait upon the Lord shall renew their strength. They shall mount up with wings like eagles.

Isaiah 40:31 TLB

Christmas In Our Hearts

It isn't far to Bethlehem town,
It's anywhere that Christ comes down,
And feels in people's smiling face,
A loving and abiding place.
The road to Bethle'm runs right through
The homes of folks like me and you.

If what you heard from the beginning abides in you, you also will abide in the Son and in the Father.
1 John 2:24 NKJV

When Christmas comes I never mind the cold.

I like to get up prompt an' go to school

An' do my sums

An' clean the walks 'thout waitin' to be told,

Though I like sleddin' better,
as a rule,

Or buildin' forts — but nothin'
ain't so bad

When Christmas comes.

— Abigail Burton, in St. Nicholas

Do good deeds all the time, for this is not only right, but it brings results.
Titus 3:8 TLB

Christmas In Our Hearts

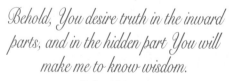

Tell me the story of Jesus,
Write on my heart ev'ry word;
Tell me the story most precious,
Sweetest that ever was heard.

— Fanny J. Crosby

Behold, You desire truth in the inward parts, and in the hidden part You will make me to know wisdom.

Psalm 51:6 NKJV

A personal Jesus accepted means salvation; a personal Jesus obeyed is sanctification; a personal Jesus followed is a life of brotherly kindness and true philanthropy; a personal Jesus reigning in the heart is the fullness of peace and joy and power. The bells of Bethlehem ring one note; the Christmas carols are all calling aloud the same note: "Back to Christ!" "Back to Christ!"

—T. L. Cuyler

Since you have been chosen by God who has given you this new kind of life...you should practice tenderhearted mercy and kindness to others.

Colossians 3:12 TLB

157

Christmas In Our Hearts

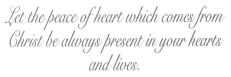

Set a chair somewhere, today, for your Master. Determine to have a Christmas all the year round, by giving your Lord and Saviour the best seat at the table in your heart.

—T. L. Cuyler

Let the peace of heart which comes from Christ be always present in your hearts and lives.

Colossians 3:15 TLB

Christmas In Our Hearts

Selfishness makes
Christmas a burden;
love makes
it a delight.

*Do unto others as you would
have them do unto you!*
Matthew 7:12 NIV

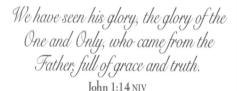

The only blind person at Christmas-time is he who has not Christmas in his heart.
— Helen Keller

We have seen his glory, the glory of the One and Only, who came from the Father, full of grace and truth.
John 1:14 NIV

References

Additional copies of this book and other titles in the
God's Little Instruction Book series are available at your local bookstore.

God's Little Instruction Book
God's Little Instruction Book II
God's Little Instruction Book — Special Gift Edition
God's Little Instruction Book for Women
God's Little Instruction Book for Men
God's Little Instruction Book for Mom
God's Little Instruction Book for Dad
God's Little Instruction Book for Couples
God's Little Instruction Book for Kids
God's Little Instruction Book for Students
God's Little Instruction Book for Graduates

Tulsa, Oklahoma